WHAT I LEARNED AT THE WAR

Poems in this collection have been previously published in *This Land, Halvard-Johnson's Truck: I-35 Creativity Corridor, Dragon Poet Review , About Place Journal, Red River Review, Yellow Medicine Review, r.k.v.r.y. Quarterly Literary Journal, Cybersoleil, Mojave River Review, San Pedro River Review, The Fiddleback, This Land, Naugatuck Review, The Dead Mule School of Southern Literature, Blast Furnace, Sexology: A Literary Journal of Sex Writing, Fried Chicken and Coffee,* and an anthology, *Trigger Warning: Poetry Saved My Life* (Swimming with Elephants, 2014).

Printed in the United States of America

First printing: March 2016

ISBN: 978-0-9910742-9-7

Typography and book design by West End Press.

Open House (cover photo) © 2015 by Jason Christian, taken near Shawnee, OK.

Inside author photo by David Bublitz.

West End Press
P.O. Box 27334
Albuquerque, NM 87125
www.westendpress.org

WHAT I LEARNED AT THE WAR

Jeanetta Calhoun Mish

West End Press

Albuquerque, New Mexico
2016

Note to the Reader
Some poems in this book have been set horizontally in order to preserve line length. Thank you for your willingness to turn the page sideways and read on.

CONTENTS

People make their own history, but they do not make it as they please; they do not make it under self-selected circumstances, but under circumstances existing already, given and transmitted from the past. The tradition of all dead generations weighs like a nightmare on the brains of the living.

—Karl Marx, from
The Eighteenth Brumaire of Louis Bonaparte

For the American Dead

But out of that silence rose new sounds more appalling still; a strange ventriloquism, of which you could not locate the source, a smothered moan, as if a thousand discords were flowing together into a key-note weird, unearthly, terrible to hear and bear, yet startling with its nearness . . . .

—Joshua Lawrence Chamberlain: 20th Maine, Army of the Potomac

1862

Here, on this field, lost voices sing strange ventriloquism.

Ventriloquism: hear estranged lost souls singing, disembodied voices.

Voices ventriloquized: a song here in ravaged trees, forever lost and strange.

Strange voices lost in ventriloquism: here, suddenly, silence sings

a song most strange—are we hearing voices? Ventriloquism utters loss.

A soldier's lost song—usurped by ventriloquism. Estranged voices haunt us here.

Here in the South, voices forever sing strange.

2015

Here in America, we forever sing strange elegies—elegies ventriloquized for the estranged and the dead. Americans sing strife, forever. Forever-elegies exported, sung off-key. Ignore sorrows of America's *stranieri* estranged forever in prisons, in graves. American elegies, everywhere, are sung. We co-opt songs of strangers. Here in our streets forever resound elegies of America. Americans sing fractured elegies—estranged, bereft, forever. Can you hear? Here—now, forever—we are afflicted—from humanity, estranged.

WHAT I LEARNED AT THE WAR

The Mice

It was late July, late afternoon,
one of those thick southern days
when shimmering heat draws a veil
over everything. A day that farmers,
eyes shaded by calloused palms or
John Deere caps, raise faces to the
stony sun and dream of rain. We tilled
the garden in March. Now, scarlet runners
weave red and green Pendletons around
their bamboo tripods, apparitions of old
Cheyenne women singing by the drum.

In her hospital room we were desperate
not to speak of death. Defying silence,
distracting her from pain, I confessed
that when running the cultivator I turned
up a nest of tiny pink, hairless mice hidden
under a zucchini's sheltering leaves. Told her
how I squatted, bawling like a child, to remove one
delicate, decapitated mouse, how I gathered
its blindly wandering siblings, tucked them back
into the earth, their mother now mewling,
quivering, inches from my bloodied hand.

We spoke of squash and mice and mothers
and of rain and scarlet runners. I tell you,
we were desperate not to speak of death.

Occupational Hazards
#1 Child Labor

No such thing as an allowance in our house—if you wanted pocket money you earned it. No payment for daily chores: bed made, trash carried out, dishes washed, table set, room cleaned and toys put away before bedtime. No payment for Saturday morning housekeeping extravaganzas, the chores assigned depending on age and height—we could have used a *you must be this tall* sign like those that guard carnival rides. Every Saturday morning without fail—no play or tv until we were done: vacuum, dust baseboards and furniture, fold laundry, knock down cobwebs with a towel-covered broom. A quarter a laundry load for ironing. I started with sheets, tablecloths, and napkins when I was ten. Burned my fingers more than once; suffered my first backache. Graduated to jeans at fifty cents a load at age eleven and developed a fetish for perfect ironed-and-starched creases. Later fell for a series of cowboys based on the perfection of their starched-and-creased pearl-button shirts and Levis. Gave up starch-and-crease when I gave up cowboys. Never ironed again.

#2 Portrait as Paramedical Roustabout

9 pm to 9 am
Friday
Saturday
Sunday
    the "diff" on hourly wages almost
    doubled my pay on 36/40 weekend shifts
    and tripled it on holidays.
I always called home, said sorry
can't be there for Christmas eve
or Easter morning
    but the truth is
    it was easier to empty
    bedpans than fight
    with my sister
more fulfilling to change
sweat-soaked sheets on a
cancer patient's bed than to
    sing gospel songs with
    my relatives, proclaiming
    a good news I didn't believe.
I felt better sliding a needle into an old
woman's blue-veined, tissue-skin hand
    than I ever did waiting for anger
    or disappointment or sorrow to erupt
    from one boyfriend or another
    and spread like smoking lava across the room.
I buzzed up on adrenalin,
pushing the EKG cart down to ER
in a rush, placing electrodes as much by feel
as by sight, moving inside a
trance-memory where all bodies became
the count and curve of left-side ribs—
    sometimes I worked the lab where
    sacred human fluids arrived sheaved
    in glass bodies or clinging to the tip
    of a swab. There, I lived in the temple
    of Isis, an acolyte of healing, learning
    chants against dismemberment.

It was easier, too,
shooting invisible rays through
little boys with broken arms and
entering into darkness afterwards
to perform alchemy, bringing ghostly
images forth from the darkest material
    than it was to cure my own disease—
    the graveyard shift and weekend schedule
    a safe haven from the rites of dating
    and sex. Except for the ER guys
and we all knew our empty-hospital-
bed assignations were nothing more
and nothing less than a spell against death,
    a spell that did not cover me when I emerged
    into the bright mornings of the mundane world
    where I could not save anyone, not even myself.

#3 Not Quite Glengarry

At 8am, my friend dropped me off in front
of a nondescript yellowish strip-mall building
at the crumbled edge of Little Rock; the parking

lot mostly empty. *People with personable voices*
needed. No experience necessary. Apply today.
I was trying to go straight, attempting to abandon

an assortment of marginally legal employments.
Hoping to land a job with only a high school
degree, two weeks after a miscarriage, one week

after my boyfriend wrecked my car, hocked all
my furniture, spent the rent money, then ran off
with his ex-wife. I believed I could change

my life by changing jobs. The lead, My Roma,
just back from *THE most motivational seminar*
EVER, lurched around the room like a speed freak

in a baby blue leisure suit that went out
of style eight years before in 1975. We
would *SELL LIKE SAMSON* (whoever

the hell that was. Perhaps My Roma thought
he was the guy who invented Samsonite).
The Outbound Telemarketing Specialist

who had been there longest, My Williamson,
handed us our scripts. *Hello, my name is Machine*
Levene and I'm calling you today because you are

the lucky winner of a set of steak knives. You don't
remember entering a drawing? You didn't—
we've chosen you from a long list of deserving

men and women who rarely catch a break
much less win a prize. You only have to pay
*for . . .*I made it half a day before an old lady

answered with a voice that sounded just like
my granny's and I couldn't bear the shame of lying
to her, of asking her to send only $49.95 in shipping

and handling charges for a set of plastic-handled
steak knives with flimsy aluminum blades, couldn't
tell her that, according to My Blake who flashed

a sample like a switchblade, they came encased
in a red velvet bag with faux silk drawstrings. I
apologized for disturbing Mrs. Somebody's Granny,

grabbed my coat and walked out. And kept walking
a mile to the nearest bus stop where I waited an hour
for the next bus. Three transfers and two hours after

embarking, I was back where I was staying with a friend
from AA. A new job had not changed my life, but it had
changed my mind about the value of employment

at all costs. The next week, I hitchhiked home
to Tulsa, couch-surfed, read Marx for the first time,
called myself *proletarian*. Never looked back.

Sometimes there was an armistice
for Coop and Dakoda

Four men, knowing I was terrified
of a formal dinner I had to attend,
(having never had much experience
with fancy events), sat me down
in the lobby of the Habana Inn
where we lived, uncased their
makeup tools, teased me about being
their token breeder while their eyes looked
past me at one of the year's Gay Miss
America contestants who had just waltzed
into the hotel's late-sixties-era faded
decadence and blinding chandeliers—all of us
here in this haven for lovers of the "wrong"
persuasion, a haven for me, too—
a battered homeless nomad in the dead
center of home. I owned nothing suitable
to wear to a literary banquet so I borrowed
a chocolate brown low-cut jumpsuit
from my mother who, for the first time
since she was 16, was carousing around
dancing her shoes thin, joyous. Her necklace,
too, a decent piece of cocktail jewelry:
square chunk of topaz glass, supported
by a thick, braided, electroplated-gold-veneer
chain that left a green spot on the back
of my neck. These four men took pity on me,
took me on as a project, told me to come
down thirty minutes before my debut—
promised to transform me from gawky
tomboy and wanna-be poet into fairy-tale
princess despite my mother's years
of utter failure at lady-making. Their mink
powder brushes blushed my cheeks,
they yanked stray brow hairs without mercy,
fretted over my bitten nails and raw cuticles.

Their manicured hands twisted my thick brown
hair into a french braid, accented by loose
tendrils curled with an iron. Iced and calmed
what was left of my most-recent black
eye. I went to the ball and, as I remember it,
managed to always use the right fork
and to not say *fuck* out loud, not even once.

Literacy Autobiography 1961-1992
#1 Body Language

My first language, mothersmell, rhythm of womb, song of glass milk bottles clanking in pot of boiling water. A child reads her mother—her true smile, her frown, the danger signal of one black eyebrow arched high above the other combined with lowering intonation in her voice. Fear, too, has its own register, one heard in greater frequency after mother married the stepfather. The wavery voice that followed the defiant one, a chord progression I mastered for myself after learning to read other bodies, male bodies. Chest puffed out like a rooster's; the crouched-to-spring-out-at-you position; the satisfied smile that arose from composing the very best method to cause a cower. The hand reaching for a belt or a long-neck bottle, the fist swinging, the leg drawn back the perfect distance to kick with accuracy. This language I have tried to forget, so as not to confuse an arm reaching out in comfort with one poised to choke; so as not to confuse a body hovering over me in ecstasy with one preparing to suffocate.

#2 Proper Punctuation

When I was in kindergarten, I fell in love with the period, that no-nonsense carbony dot of punctuational closure. Ironic, for a girl—later, I would moan "I hate my period" but of course, I didn't mean the sentence-ending kind. My love affair with Mssr. P was inextricably related to my fling with the sentence— I could read and write when I arrived in Mrs. Dunlap's lemon-polished classroom, but had not yet enticed a pearly string of words to join together in holy meaning. Before the afternoon I wrote "Sam ran fast" on my Big Chief tablet, I was innocent of my need for the period, but it soon became an obsession. It seemed to me that Sir Period had power to put a full stop to overwhelming demands, to end entire families of caustic words, to insist *no more* and be taken seriously. I lingered with Period, blunting my pencils and poking holes in paper while retracing each one to its deepest possible blackness. Every period gleamed with excess graphite, the fingers on my writing hand stained, the side of my palm slick from slogging through lead slag heaps on the way to the next sentence, the next opportunity to create another singularity of imagined infinite density, not a black hole but a worm hole into another world where King Period reigned supreme. A world where chaos was contained between periods, exclamation points were always gleeful, and question marks were nothing to fear. When I was older, I transferred my affections to the semicolon. I could not abandon the period entirely but desired a more flexible, functional punctuator, one that could divide and conjoin, end and begin, simultaneously.

#3 To Have It By Heart

Which was first? Twinkle Twinkle? Hickory Dickory? Humpty Dumpty or Rockabye Babe? By the time I was 6 I had 20 or more by heart. Not *knew* by heart, *had*, possessed, claimed, owned. Later, church songs: Sunday morning organ songs— formal chords, overwrought metaphors—and Sunday evening piano gospel songs and spirituals in minor keys, downhome, composed by Anon. Folk songs and children's songs, more clocks, some eerie canal, green sleeves and blue bells and red river valley. But it was Poe, his dead and haunted, his hypnotic rhythms and creepy scenes that looped silently in my ears on Friday and Saturday nights in cars with fathers of children I babysat, while their zippers wheezed, while I choked and gasped and didn't cry. While windows fogged and through them the neighborhood surrealed and my tell-no-tale-heart-in-mouth tasted like ash.

#4 To Have It By Heart, Part 2

when in ER for psych eval:
      Lorca's "Canción del Jinete"
(well, doc said, mumble mumble mumble)
      How long the road
(bipolar, personality disorder, psychotic break)
      Death is looking at me
(take this pill, stop screaming, don't fight)
      Far away and alone

when homeless:
      Sandburg's "The Road and the End"
all night diner on crackers, ketchup & two
cups of coffee. 5am dawns cloudy—an
unlocked car in corporate lot—back seat
beckons. nothing to lose but desolate dreams
      The broken boulders by the road
      Shall not commemorate my ruin.

when hungry:
      Hernandez' "Lullaby of the Onion"
map out by day of week all happy hours
serving free food. go to poetry readings
and art openings as much for the meatballs
and strawberries as for soul-sustenance.
learn 5 ways to hack 59¢ a box mac & cheese,
imagine angels bringing french bread basted
with butter and filled with burgundy roses.
drink water, taste wine. consume stars,
      black ice and frost
      you can swallow the moon

when scared:
 Harjo's "I Give You Back"
of darkness. of pain. of hunger. of
fear itself. shadows, raised fists, torn
dresses. the small light under the door.
 I release you
of being lost. of being found. of finding
a lump, losing a mind. of dying. of not dying.
of ruthless rooms in sad motels. of myself.
 I release you
of rattling soul & silent heart.
 I release you.

#5 Practical Uses for Writing
an exhibition catalogue, 1961-1979

Cartouche: footprint impression. Black ink on birth certificate, 1961.

Mother's Day card inscriptions, from author to author's mother. Crayon, pencil, pen; circa 1965-1979; complete collection archives cards to 2009.

Valentine addressed and signed by author. Returned to sender, unopened; in fragile condition, crumpled. 1968(?).

First known poem, untitled. Subject matter: witnessing death of dog by feral dog pack attack. Big Chief tablet paper; thumbtack holes in corners, yellowed, 1969.

Handwritten messages. Large collection on torn and folded notebook paper, wide-ruled and college-ruled. Some addressed to "Sammye," "Elizabeth," "Travis," "Tim," and other recipients; most unaddressed. Circa 1969-1975.

Postcards from Camp Waluhili, Chouteau, OK. 50 +/- pieces addressed to "Momma" and "Granny and Grandpa." Subjects: among others, canoeing, archery, tent city, mean girls, rapes/ murders in adjoining camp. Circa 1969-1977.

Two shoeboxes of correspondence. Of note, letter from and drafts of letters to Isaac Asimov. Others unremarkable. Circa 1974-1976.

Poem, "My First Time," published in *Wewoka Daily Times* as winner of high school poetry contest. March 1976.

School absence excuse slip, signed by author's mother; handwriting comparisons indicate forgery by author. October 1977.

Patient treatment record with notation of positive pregnancy test, signed by author. Planned Parenthood of Norman, OK. January 7, 1978.

Acknowledgment of side effects of Ortho-Novum, signed by author's mother; handwriting comparisons indicate forgery by author. February 28, 1978.

Letter to J.S. regarding her move to San Francisco and possibility of author relocating there. August 1978.

Handwritten application for National Merit Scholarship, November 1978.

Copy of signed form declining partial scholarship to Brown University, March 31 1979.

Release of Personal Items from Wewoka Police Department, signed by author. May 4, 1979.

Handwritten draft of Salutatorian's Graduation Speech, May 10, 1979.

Wewoka High School yearbook, signed by author on yearbook/newspaper staff photo, May 23, 1979.

Southwest Airlines reservation receipt for one-way flight to Houston, Texas, with poem fragment inscribed on reverse. June 1, 1979.

#6 A Short Glossary of Useful Acronyms

AEDs

Anti-Epileptic Drugs used as mood stabilizers for bipolar disorder. Not to be confused with IEDs, although they have a similar effect on the brain. Example: Depakote

BAD

Bipolar Affective Disorder. The diagnosis you get instead of PTSD when your MMPI (see MMPI) has *A large number of F Scale items . . . endorsed,* and, therefore, *The profile's validity is questionable.* This means they think you're lying about or, at the very least, exaggerating the abuse and violence. However, lying is not a word you will hear come out of your therapist's mouth. S/he might say, however, that your MMPI suggests you are *malingering* or *pleaing* (sic.) *for help.*

BPD

Borderline Personality Disorder. Another diagnosis you get when they think you're lying about the abuse and the violence, especially when your Personality Assessment Inventory indicates you have *little regard for* bourgeois *social standards and values* and that you are *cynical about human nature and suspicious of other peoples' motives.* Cynicism and suspicion of others' motives, no matter how well-founded, is pathological. Keep this in mind when seeking help.

FGAs

First Generation Antipsychotics like Haldol. They will fuck you up and not in a good way.

MMPI

The Minnesota Multiphasic Personality Inventory, a test often used in combination with the Personality Assessment Inventory, the Clinical Analysis Questionnaire, and the Incomplete Sentence Blank. Despite designers' claims, it can be manipulated by certain intellectually adept patients to help their therapists feel like they've done their job.

PTSD

Post Traumatic Stress Disorder, a common malady of working class and poor women and children. Can be repurposed as mnemonic for emotional and drug rehab: *Put That Shit Down.*

SSRIs

Selective Serotonin Reuptake Inhibitors, a class of antidepressants (Zoloft, Paxil, Prozac). Infamous for causing agitation and aggression, while, at the same time, relieving depression just enough that patients find the energy to attempt suicide.

#7 What I Learned at the War

The price of your body is directly inverse to whatever is valuable.

Never let a man you don't know bring you a drink in a sleazy bar. This is an international rule: in the not-yet-former-but-certainly-crumbling-Yugoslavia, it was belladonna; in West Tulsa, chloral hydrate (AKA Micky Finn).

Bullets do less damage when they enter you from point blank range. It's physics. Ask your local gun enthusiast.

Scars sunburn easily when they're fresh. When they're no longer red-raw, you can't see them anymore although others do.

Don't chase a man down dark streets with a loaded revolver in your hand while wearing his friend's size 12 Chucks. The stumbling screws up your aim.

It is possible to drown in your own blood. Sit up. You might have a chance.

Kidney shots hurt worse than cracked ribs hurt worse than black eyes hurt worse than clumps of hair pulled out hurt worse than taking out a restraining order.

A restraining order is more dangerous than leaving town, even if you have nowhere to go and have to sleep in a shelter in a strange city. Sometimes he'll mistake it for a hunting license.

Never walk out the door of a bar without checking for someone lying in wait, especially when a woman just out of prison knows you been sleeping with her ex while she did her time. Ex means nothing to a woman doing 5 years.

Large scars on young women make bougie strangers nervous. Make use of this.

Know thyself: if getting sucker punched from behind the door of a bar or your tit twisted on the dance floor by your trash bro-in-law sends you into a blind rage, make sure to have good friends with you at all times. Buying their drinks is less expensive than attempted murder.

Never go to bail out your ex-con boyfriend when you have an unpaid traffic ticket. He's out! You're in. You just spent your last dime springing him and he doesn't have a job.

If you must self-medicate, choose the right drug: meth for depression, coke for low self-esteem, opiates for pain of the physical & existential sort. Weed for whatever ails you. Psychedelics to soothe spiritual alienation. Alcohol if you can't afford anything better.

Try not to think about whether there is somewhere no war is going on. It's like sending happy postcards to your former pimp in prison—it just makes the situation more unbearable.

Recovery

Just last month I was forced to sacrifice
My Muse on the altar of Our Relationship
and today I read that poets must also give up
the "Confessional I"—it has become irrelevant
and self-indulgent. It is also recommended
that one wean oneself from the "Lyric I"
as it does not address the postmodern, posthuman,
world—the "Witness I" might, in some poems,
remain admissible although suspect.
I'm working on it . . . it's difficult to give up
one's Muse and one's I's in the same year.
I'm attending meetings, working the steps—
I've made formal amends for having a Muse
who is not my significant other, cut off all email
messages and promised to stop looking toward
the northwest. My Muse-dry date is June 29
and I am now a recovering Muse-user
a recovering I-poet, a recovering alcoholic
a recovering addict. My mind is flooded
in clear white light that eliminates
any sublimely obscure corners.
My inner-self is an IKEA catalogue
bleached clean, angular, and bereft of any
indication of lingering romanticism:
this subject position is now
obsession, addiction, and poetry-free.
They call this a good recovery.

Declaration of a New Poetics

From this day forward
let there be no more abstractions
nor disembodied sighs
I proclaim a new poetics rising up,
flaming out from my body as if
I were the kiln and you the potter
who flung open the door.

From now on I shall speak
only the language of the sensuous,
the sensual, the reality of
taste—touch—smell—
sight is too tricky, too easily seduced
and hearing is reliable only when
applied to the code of *ohs* and *ahs* that
cannot be mistaken or misconstrued.

The practice of my new poetics
requires that I run my tongue
along your hip, grasp your stony calves,
inhale deeply at every dark conjunction of limbs.
This poetics demands I ban every pretense,
all talk of love and questions of propriety.
It allows only this primal sacred performance
this paean to need, this clashing of bodies.

In this dangerous intriguing encounter
we open ourselves to the edge
to this honesty the body knows
to our poem of desire.

Thirst

I was born of water, to water,
but live in the desert—the cholla, the
mountain's granite spires, the Apache
plume, the piñons, still yet not home.
Not humid. Not swampy. Not thick with
sweltery intimacy. Monsoon showers
rare this year, the tv turned off to listen
to thrumming rain upon the roof.

On the front porch facing the storm,
half a second between lightning strike
and thunder. I should be in the moment,
should absorb this rain-blessed breeze
slowly, deliberately . . . I thirst for it.

But all I can think of is you—
how wet I was, how stunning
the moment, how delicate your
kisses fell on the back of my neck,
my hair twisted up in your fingers, lifted
away to make room for your mouth—
how strange that the word *delicate*
should appear in a poem for you.

I would send you this memento,
but just yesterday you praised me
for my restraint in all things emotional
and I would not want to disappoint
or disquiet you. Instead, I'll hide these
words in my body, bring them as gifts,
and hope that you, unsuspecting, might inhale
them as if they were nothing but damp night air.

Elemental Ceramics: An Imaginary Textbook
for Dainis Pundurs

Earth
is the essential element
from which we birth new forms.
You must come to know the porcelain body
as intimately as you know your lover's—
learn to recognize its attributes, its
responsiveness to the ministrations of your
hands, its tendency to grotesque malformation.
Leave it pure and white, or adorn it in metallic
finery, cobalt, copper, chrome and manganese,
adulterate it with horsehair and grog—it has given
itself to you; you accept the responsibility
for bringing it into beauty.

Water
is the hidden element of plasticity,
surface tension shuffling the deck of
silica cards, the magic of electromagnetism,
strong as love, binding earth even in
its absence. Exiled by fire and air, it is
memorialized in the vessel's curves.

Air
is the invisible element that precipitates
the exodus of water. Evaporation moves
molecules into sky. In the kiln, dancing with fire,
pressured whirlwinds desiccate and solidify.
Memory invigorated by breath. Exhalation
becomes exaltation as crystals weep.

Fire
is the transmuting element, the
techne, the gift of an ingenious god.
Bone ash and silica sintered into
strength and translucence; death
vitrified and resurrected, singing
in the soprano voice of glass.

Quintessence
is the maker's element, the spirit,
the desire that brings all things into
being, translated by hands and heart. A
master ceramicist may be recognized in the
moment when it is unclear if the artist is becoming
the vessel or the vessel is devouring its maker.

Memory with Ruby Beads

A toddler in a pink dress peers
through a long strand of ruby
beads at her father, fractured
and red, soon to be gone forever

and hears her mother, laughing.

An old woman with gray hair
and support hose offers sweating
tumblers of iced tea in the
shrinking late afternoon light.

Sunbeams whirl like dervishes
spun by the child's hand—
spreading shadows hide secrets
in the middle of the room.

Honed

Twice a year until I turned ten, the tinker
came round to my grandparents' farm
and all sharp things would arise like souls
from their sepulchers to await their reckonings
at the stone wheel. Scissors, shears, and snips:
sewing, pinking, tin, and more. Knives of all kinds:
carving, paring, fishing. Butcher, cleaver, pocket, pen.
I crouch beside them, mesmerized by wheel's
whirl, by somersaulting sparks. Covering my ears
against the great screeching whine, imagining that,
by his magic, the tinker transmitted to steel his manic
concentration, the wheel's violent devotion. Knives
transmuted into talismans, scissors charmed, dark
fairytales spun under the black oak in the side yard.

A Letter to My Cousin, Janna Little Ryan

> In all this consideration, we have so far ignored the
> white workers of the South and we have done this
> because the labor movement ignored them and the
> abolitionists ignored them; and above all, they were
> ignored by Northern capitalists and Southern
> planters. They were in many respects a forgotten
> mass of men.
>
> —W.E.B. DuBois
> *Black Reconstruction in America*

Dear Janna,

I was thinking of you today while
reading DuBois, wondering if you knew
of these people, our people, unreconstructed
southern whites, among them two orphaned
brothers who, in ironic happenstance
were raised by their Uncle Sam.
Have you heard of those boys—
Sterling Price and Luther Rice Little—
their eyes hard, their jaws
clenched, their backs stiff as their
starched Sunday shirts. The elder,
named for a desperate Confederate general
his father and Grandfather Venable served;
the younger, not yet born
the afternoon his father was murdered,
named after a Southern Baptist evangelist.

Our forgotten men and their families strode
out of the primordial muck of Arkansas
river bottoms driven by poverty,
hunger, and their grandfather's exile:
Grandpa Theophilus, as his name befits,
had argued with his father over the slave question,
argued that negroes were humans and not
to be owned. Leaving the Georgia Piedmont,
fingering the buckeye in his front pocket,
Theo lit out for Indian Territory with his young
Cherokee wife, but, shaking sick
with the ague, pulled up the paired
gray mules in Van Buren County

Arkansas where his son was murdered,
where his raven-haired grandsons were born—

Sterling stayed in Arkansas. Luther
headed for North Texas. Both
were stricken by forgetfulness: Sterling
swore out an affidavit declaring
his ancestors were *pure anglo-saxon*.
Luther was drawn to drink despite
his dying mother's prayers and his uncle's
Calvinist discipline. Forgotten, too,
Theo's steadfast refusal of planter's
privilege that cost him all
but five dollars from his father's estate.

Do you ever wonder how it came
to be that those barely-white-boys'
daughters' ears were stained with
nigger; their great-grand-daughters'
elegant red lips grown
accustomed to spitting the word?

Like their great-granddaughter—
my mother—who said *colored*
in public except for one of her last days
in the chemo room when she pondered aloud
why that beautiful woman went and married that nigger
her bony finger jabbing each beat
on a magazine photo of Heidi Klum.
My response not strong enough, cowed
by her fragility, her impending death.

Do you wonder, Cousin, why the word
tastes foul in my mouth but didn't
in my mother's? Only my stubborn
vow not to accept my cockfight-going,
nigger-hating, *kike*-hating, *spic*-hating,

Klannish stepfather. Nothing noble.
Just hatred of another kind.

Why should we speak of those brothers now, Cousin?
Sterling named for war, Luther for religion,
descended from Ulster Scots who were bribed
with land and and constrained freedom
to displace their Irish kin? Those
brothers and their ilk who removed
their Indian in-laws. Who burned out
their Black neighbors' homes.
Whose sons still ridicule the poor.

Another war between sons and fathers,
mothers and daughters,
rumbles underground, deep pools
of hatred bubbling up like Indian
Territory oil, pressured to the surface
by fear of a Black man in the White
House, by the clamoring of the poor and
forgotten, the insistent claims to humanity . . .

Tell me, Janna, must we meet
on the battlefield, recognize each other as kin,
loading our rifles in the enemy camp,
just before the bullets fly?

What Sarah Venable Little Told the Sheriff
May 1863, Lockesburg, Arkansas

I came out to bring his dinner
just a biscuit full of bacon and butter
and a tin cup of cold water from the well.
Our boy Sterling Price was napping on a featherbed
in the fresh air and shade of the east porch.

I was slow at fixing our midday meal,
so awkward and worn out, so full with child—
any other day I would have come round the barn
in time to see who done it, but as it was
all I noticed was dust flying down the road a ways.

John, I called, but he did not answer; he was fond
of fooling with me but I was in no mood for fun.
John, I hollered, *don't toy with me, I brought
your dinner and I am hot and tired and now the
baby is crying.* But he did not answer still.

I shaded my eyes and looked out over the field.
No John, and no horses, neither. When I spied
the plow laid over I thought maybe he had
taken the horses down to the creek for a drink.
Thinking to set the plow aright, I went over that way.

It was his leg I saw first, caught up in the plow—
My John. My God
I thought that when he come back from the war
I would have no more to worry about, but there
he lay, the brown shirt I just mended covered in blood
and him reaching out to me with a quivering hand.

His lips were moving but he had not breath
enough to call out to me; his eyes were darting
about, frantic, like those of a startled horse.
I sat beside him, put his head in my lap, kissed
his salty cheek and heard his last word: *carpetbaggers.*

What Sarah Venable Little Wrote in Her Diary
May 1866, Lockesburg, Arkansas

Dear sons,

Try my best, I can't put off my dying
any longer, the Lord calls, and I must go,

leaving you orphans of an orphan—
my mother dead just last month

my father dead in this accursed war
that has taken so many

your father dead of fruits of this war
murdered in his own fields.

I leave you to your uncle Sam
over to the next county he

is the only one left who
has means to care for you.

I pray that one day you will
take up my words and read them,

that you will read these words
heed them and repent.

I cannot help but believe
this dying all around us

is God's great wrath come down
on your father's family and mine

because we turned away from
our grandmothers' simple faith

forgot the commandment
to never take up arms against another.

We are covered in blood unrepentant.
We have sinned sinned sinned.

We spill the blood
of the poor Indians in their fields.

We put the lash to the bloody backs
of the Negroes in the fields.

We murder our kin
in the fields of war.

Here in these bloody fields
we have sown your orphanage.

So shall you reap that which you sow—
This, too, is God's promise to his children.

Honor your mother's dying words,
swear upon your father's bloody field:

We repent of our family's sins
and will go and sin no more.

Holding the Unspeakable

Lately, there is too much time in the past—Ancestry.com,
mother's perfume riding wind through open window.
On Facebook, Hometown People plant nostalgia bombs.

Twenty-five years ago, a girl slept on Isola d'Elba beach
and woke envying Napoleon's banishment.

Once, the girl escaped a Schenectady tavern, back door into
yellow alley, fleeing lover who tried kill her but later old white
man chewing pipe behind long dark desk said *no,
just a psychotic break.*

There is never a moment
when love is enough to tell the truth.

The shame of admitting that death-of-choice
was once methamphetamine.

The shame of returning home from baptism preparation class
sprinkled with preacher's semen in direct contradiction
to church's insistence on immersion.

The guilt of waking from recurring dreams—murdering,
hiding bodies. She cannot see the faces of the dead.
Fears it is a memory not a dream.

Builds a form framed with 2x4s, pours cement of shame
mixed with guilt-and-fear aggregate, uses it as foundation.

A legion of army ants break formation, scattering frantic
across foundation, searching for cookie-crumb-trail
home through the trees.

The Weight

two silvered base metal
belt buckles, his letter S
engraved, estimate 4
ounces apiece humming
bird heft. edges sharp
as grief.

black handled bowie
knife, yearbook '76,
two handbuilt dream
catchers, pyrographic
leather belt his finest
writing. his heart
a feather's balance.

black white and tan woven
fabric hand bag, cordovan
wallet, prescription bottle—
5 tiny explosions inside—
convert objects' mass
to 21 grams, her last
goodbye.

That Summer...

in remembrance: Lori Lee Farmer, Doris Denise Milner, & Michele Guse, victims of the 1977 Oklahoma Girl Scout murders.

... was strange, an anomaly, a bad movie
suddenly real. Did the cute dumb girl die first?
The news shimmered and shook, rocked our world
like never before. But the ghosts of Chouteau

were stronger than an earthquake, that old
camp with its log cabins built looming
over an night-heron haunted lake
the woods behind dark as a serial-killer's heart.
We shivered in our tents while you died in yours.

How could I have known the north star
whispered a dark secret to the wind—
how could I have known the ghosts heard
it, too? Home, now, a great horned owl hoots
outside my window, summoning the moon.

Elegy for My First Boyfriend
Shawn Mart Powell, 11/1/1961-3/26/76

Just kids, awkward, both of us. You a country
boy, sweet, honest. You asked your brother's girl to
deliver silver roadrunner necklace, too shy
        to ask me yourself.

Girlfriend! Me! For first time, that blasted blighted
spring of Seventy-six, and you, late home when
down a red road brother saw father's tractor.
        Upside down. Reaper

come to take you away and I, lost among
hundreds at your funeral, slipped a silver
bird in casket. No one knew. I'm ashamed this
        elegy's so late.

When Dreams Die

a golden shovel after "truth" by Gwendolyn Brooks

One gray morning, the gasping of What
will wake us from secondhand sleep. If
will soon follow, claiming the conjugal We
of their syntactically inseparable wake—
upon demise of What, If sits keening by one
brassed pine box, chasing soul-shimmering
transcendence, the dawn of inward-morning—
conditionals and suppositions serve supper to
our bereft unsayable dreams. Listen! Hear
humming of hymns, wailing of women, the
banal benediction in future's falsetto, fierce
fists beating breasts, the final hammering.

Malissa, 1983

A week before, I bought my first
maternity gear at the Goodwill,
a brown empire-waist polyester
top with tiny pink flowers,
necessity overruling my
puritan sense of style.

You are a piece of tattered pink
lace clinging to a descanso
on a dirt road to nowhere. A
roadside in my mind. A place
we never were. A place you
might be now, alone.

Your father who left me a week
after, who stranded me alone in
Little Rock without you, drove us
to the hospital in my yellow '76
Super Beetle, yelled at the nurses
to find a wheelchair—

You are a shard of black glass
stuck in my heart. You are the silly
faces I make at other people's babies
in restaurants and grocery stores.

Named for a song and after a
great-grandmother whose middle
name was a river. You felt like
a waterfall down my thigh, in
my chest. You felt like a stitch
in my side. It was your first
and only cry.

You are the yellow wing
on a dark bird that soars
toward the sun. I lose you
to spots in my eyes.

My Mother's Hands

It was not the silk-lined coffin or the mewling
of Muzaked hymns that set me off . . .
It was not her closed eyes.
It was not her closed lips and the ritual lipstick
that was for the first time ever the wrong color . . .
It was not the suddenly apparent age lines in her neck
that my sister and I concealed beneath a favorite cerulean scarf,
knowing that she would have been *just mortified.*

It was her hands, the color of three day old orange peels,
the swollen purses of sagging skin between index and thumb.

My mother's nails had always been perfect, painted
the color of sunset, a tint that would *go with most everything.*
Emery boards stood on her dresser like ready soldiers
defending against nicks and snags; her cuticles trimmed and
oiled to smooth out the day's labor. Creamy white and blue-
veined as the gorgonzola she'd come to love, her hands
were always gloved when weeding or pruning, protected
from the garden sun because *that's how the ladies do it.*

Those could not be her hands. Her hands had never been still.

Room for Aunt Pearl

> I thought about the organ booming in the chapel
> and of the shut doors of the library; and I thought
> how unpleasant it is to be locked out; and I thought
> how it is worse perhaps to be locked in
> —Virginia Woolf
> *A Room of One's Own*

the sun, moon and morning star in cobalt
glass, poems spilling out of shelves onto
the window sill, the desk, the floor
5 marble eggs and Groucho Marx ...

Above my desk
Great-Aunt Pearl's painting
of wisteria in periwinkle
bloom, rising from a brass pot

crystal teardrops, small smooth stones,
exquisitely thin envelopes—palest blue,
amber sealing wax, postcards from Germany
and Italy and Spain ...

My Aunt Pearl who was like me
certified and medicated,
intriguing dangerous opal fire

an untamable woman
an unnameable desire

overflowing rolodex, mementos of old
lovers, playbills, concert stubs—Bob Dylan
and Brahms, Memphis Minnie on CD ...

Having spent her friends and family
Aunt Pearl died alone, drunk
and drugged and demented, destitute—
in a claustrophobic shack-trailer, west Odessa,
flies buzzing against the screen, bumping
for a turn at the five-day-old corpse ...

filigree pearl centered cross, medicine wheel
necklace, earrings for Día de los Muertos, tarot
cards, incense, candles thick . . .

come home, Aunt Pearl,
bring your aspect here to my room
of mystery and magic, splintered
by the tiniest mote of gold

an open hand, your genes expressed
and embraced, a vision to match your own.

1977, Seminole County

Me and my best friend K.T. hurtled down
chug-holed roads in her green Gran Torino,
racing almost as fast as our doped up hearts,
our hysterical laughter counter-pointed by the crash
of glass on rural mailboxes, my aim truer
after killing a bottle of Night Train Express
guzzled over ice in a Sonic cup.
We wanted our lives
to go fast but every Sunday morning
strung-out and sore-jawed, we confessed
that all the crank in the world could
not give us the escape velocity we needed
while making plans to try again
on Thursday, just the same.

A Message for Stephanie

Stephanie, whoever you are,
your brother called about 9:15 pm
from the bar. You know which bar,
it's the one he flees to when
he *just can't take this shit anymore.*

He was already *pretty damn toasted,*
misdialed the number by one clumsy digit,
left the message on my phone instead of yours.
Didn't notice the answering machine
announced a strange name.

Stephanieeeee, call me.
It's your brother. Clunk.

Whatever else you do this evening,
when he calls again—and we both know he will—
call him back.

Or I will, hoping that my brother
will pick up from the last bar in the universe
where he's just placed the same call
and he's *pretty damn sure* that this one time
my disapproval is less important than his despair.

The Unexplored Prairie

> the flies & musquitoes abound in summer—in the
> spring the streams are high & the mud deep—and
> later in the fall the immense praries are on fire, to
> destroy both man & beast.
>
> —Henry Leavitt Ellsworth
> *Washington Irving on the Prairie: Or, a Narrative*
> *of a Tour of the Southwest in the Year 1832*

Summer
safe on my grandparents' farm
no *cannabals*, no broken furniture.
Indulgent imaginings that my
mother wasn't crying silently
into her 7 & 7 by 8 o'clock.
No need to dodge science
teacher's groping hands—
Entire days spent roaming
the farm, dreaming of
boarding school, of leaving.
A girl mesmerized by
gnat clouds, their morphing
flight, *flies* brushed
away by horse's tail.
Musquitoes' whining buzz
punctuated by the scream
of the last cougar
in Seminole County.

Fall
Prairie *fires* a distant
memory signaled on humid
nights by dying
fireflies' last messages.
Return to school and sorrow,
escapes limited to rare
weekends. The *beast* is the *man*
my mother married. All
of us destroyed, my brother first.
I became a desperate
romantic, lying awake at
midnight in my room

at the farm, wishing my soul
into the great horned owl
eating june bugs
under the vapor lamp,
wishing on the first faint
star that I'd never have to
go back home.

Spring
brought a week of respite
ruined by Easter
Sunday egg hunt,
stained by my stepfather's
angry barking and cigarette
smoke rings—by my brother's
tears, until he moved in
with our grandparents and I, bereft,
having then no partner in resistance,
stared out my window
into interminable gray sheets
of rain, measuring the rising
streams against my fear
and all of us, human and animal
alike trapped in the season
of diseases, the season of red
mud thick enough
to suck the boots off
our wandering feet.

Winter
Ellsworth, no romantic
like Irving, instead a practical
man who deemed early
winter the best season
for crossing unexplored
prairies, riding through
knife-edged crosstimbers
bare and black against

stark faded sky.
No bugs, no fires, no rain,
only the dark and the beasts
and you.
           But I cannot
go in winter, can not
make myself explore
mother's broken jaw,
brother's humiliation, the
hours we were locked out,
quivering on the front porch
in the snow, the monstrous voice
behind the door telling
us to run away.
           Winter
is no time for exploring
the prairie, not this
prairie, not this *immense*
forsaken *prarie* where
even now my heart
pounds like that of the young
Duke in Ellsworth's company,
who, lost after a buffalo hunt,
climbed a tree to escape
the night and the howling wolves.
The Duke was found the next morning
by his companions, alive and whole.

My brother drank and died
young. I was found alive.

Pastoral for My Brother

Today, I remember
prowling the woods with you
smashing wild grapes
into our haunted mouths,
smoking the vines.

You ran faster, your spindly
three-years-older boy legs
bounding across a darkening
field, my seven-year-old shadow
racing ahead of me, grasping
for your boots as if it longed
to be stitched to your heels.

Where woods joined
pasture, a meadowlark, alarmed
by our laughter, squawked, dragged
her spotted wing in decoy, her chicks
betrayed the grave game with laughter
of their own. In the gully,
among years of refuse, you
found a marriage plate broken
in half, separating our mother
and your father as surely
as the divorce. A week later,
I destroyed your newly-mended
memento, threw the shattered
porcelain pieces into the lake.

I do not remember why.

The meadowlark still drags
her wing. The shadows
are even longer, reaching
for you where I cannot go.

Arroyo Piño
for Kyran

Hiking up the arroyo, we stop often to gaze
down at the yolk-yellow ribbon of cottonwoods
lacing the Bosque. We have never been young
together so we go deliberately, yearnings
tempered by years and experience.

We pause near a cholla cactus, yielding
to its scarlet blossoms and besotted
bees. You pull me me toward you, kiss
me deeply. The piñons blush. We return
to the uphill trail, following scent of
yarrow and yammering of jays.

Dirt

After Gwendolyn Brooks, "The Bean Eaters"

This red soil
built of blood sweat
and promises.

This red soil
the soil that looks
the soil of centuries

makes you remember
where you come from
where you be going.

Makes you wish
you never learned
the wrong words—

the words that mark
you as cracker although
your heart is not.

Oh, red soil
make us instead
remember

the sacrifices—
our grandmothers'
poverty,

our grandfathers'
despair, their
native exile.

Centuries lost
to one another
yet in the light

behind the bar—
in which every
one is blue—

whoever
stands beside you
offering

is your brother
and your sister
of the soil.

Barn

leaning on a rounded hill
waving to buzzards
what's left of an old red
A-frame barn soars upward,
a cathedral of loss, a
shelter for mice and
possums and maybe
a rare tawny-eyed bobcat
whose kittens are tucked
under the rotting manger.
witness the gaping hayloft,
sweep your eyes down
to slovenly underbrush—
here is a thing like a jar
that makes the world
rise up and call out—
a skeletal frame to rein in
undulating miles of sky
which would otherwise be
more than we could bear.

Barefoot Philosophy

Out here with the warm dark earth
squishing up between my toes
I'm fearless. Not even the lime green
horned tomato worm scares me although
it rears up like a wounded dragon.

Yet there are dangers everywhere: the yoyo
blade too close to my foot and like
the reaper's scythe it momentarily
becomes a metaphor instead of a tool.

A pygmy rattler lives under the squash
blossoms and when I walk by carrying
a bag of of bone meal, she hisses as if
the ashes of the dead were calling out.

Even the fruits of the garden are risky—
sanguine tomatoes are perilous nightshades,
peach pits have poisonous hearts, and the poke
sallet that has sprung up between the lilac bush
and the Rose of Sharon whispers constantly that
he is most delicious when blanched only once. He's
such a liar, but I know his ways. I am at home
in the garden, and the perils here are comforting,
real. Understandable. Ancient. Reciprocal.

I know my place and my part. What I'd give
to make of the world a garden, again.

Ode to Psilocybe

Every spring when raging rainstorms were
followed by warm days and nights, southern style,
proud in manure you grew, *Psilocybe
cubensis,* magic mushroom, bounty of
rich earth, golden crowns rising to greet us—
blessed, harvested, dried, shared with those of like
mind. Our communion, friendships' bitter seal.
Cleansed doors of perception revealed to us
spiders' subtle eggs, infinite worlds, our
hidden inheritance, saffron courage.

It has been years, old friend, since we last met
on my thirtieth birthday, but I swear
I hear you, Maecenas of the pasture,
singing blank verse odes in ebony nights,
calling me to return to damp dark fields,
to pull on my boots, to venture into
meadows wet with yesterday's rain, to turn
four times around before scanning the ground.
To find *there,* by my right foot, another
clarity—a path home at this late hour.

Deep Center
a double tanka

I am pebble thrown
down a rock well, monolith's
daughter, crude cousin
to etched limestone, the
lithographer's tool—

a somber boulder
bounding down dappled ashlight
toward origin—
seek ancestors' deep center—
redemption: melting, merging.

On the Neosho

vapor lamps
illuminate
dead
shumard oak's
riven skin

foxes scream
then suddenly
the woods are still

in rough crotch
of black walnut
a lightning bug
looks for all the world
like a hot spark
freshly struck

from the flint
of a single bright star
barely visible
through darkening
canopy

Susquehanna Dreams
for Susan, David, Lucy, & Grace

1.
The longest river in New England winds its way
through the valley below, girding the hillside's thick waist.
Woodpeckers thrum tall lilting trees.

2.
Tell me, wordless young woman, what you know.
Your black eyes challenge the universe.
I surrender before your mute wisdom.

3.
Susan, sister to Susquehanna, you speak for the land
like you speak of our kin. The old names that remain are
everywhere a rebuke to a people who have no history.

4.
In a room at the top of the stairs, a gentle man dreams
the secrets of the universe. The music of his star-
desire is sung by jesters and kings.

5.
On an April day when spring seems tardy, a child
discovers a single red tulip. She dances,
sure of regeneration and her parents' delight.

6.
I will take your hearts home
with me, smooth river stones
embraced in the palm of my hand.

Fish Wisdom

Signs everywhere:
House of Tomorrow
opens its door
as I stroll by
when you need answers
in purple paint
on the window
of the psychic's hut
a dove asks *who*
are you who are you
while a magpie cackles.

At the koi pond,
just as I wonder
how fish know
food from flotsam,
a sapphire-scaled old
woman-fish rises,
gulps, swims
two strokes, then
opens her mouth
expelling not-food.

Take it in.
Take it all in,
release what
does not nourish.
What remains is
who you are.

Mea Culpa

I am becoming an old woman whose imagination is harnessed
to a sentimental horse and so I mourn for you, women I loved

and lost through cowardice. Like you, Samantha, your wiry black hair
purpled under Hendrix-poster blacklights in the corner of the bar

we were neither one old enough to frequent. I touched you
first in the graffitied bathroom when you asked me to *please*

put my earring back in—for three months we met at your house,
washed each other's backs, braided hair, made love awkwardly,

not having pleasured women before. I don't (want to) remember
if I left you or if, together, we decided it was best, because neither

of us Oklahoma small-town girls could bear the shame of an invisible
scarlet L emblazoned on our backs or risk pain of a real one, branded

on an arm by a redneck with a hot coat hanger. No acts of contrition can
cleanse my selfish gutlessness because I knew that two summers before,

my lifelong best friend cleaned shoepolished *lesbo* and *cuntmuncher*
off her pickup before driving her girl to the City. I still dream of you,

Samantha, of you and four other women who loved me
	better than I loved you or myself.

Forgive me, I call out to you as you take a laughing girl's hand
	and disappear into blue sky.

Driving Lost Roads Listening to Jedi Mind Tricks: A Ghazal
For James

I'm once in a life time Haley's Comet out here
Gods, and Earth's, and Moors we Islamic out here.
  from "Chalice" by Vinnie Paz, Jedi Mind Tricks

  oklahoma will be the last song
  i'll ever sing.
    from "the last song" by Joy Harjo

We all know there is only one road home; no other choice out here, *You cannot be located, cannot be located,* insists the haughty GPS voice. Out here, you cannot be.

We see no other people for hours; all things man-made corrode into monuments of dread. Nothing is louder than prophesied silence. Souls recoil, out here, where *anything* might be.

Just past a ghost town's melancholy edge, old possum sits staring at a red-spotted toad. Fresh branches top the arbor at Mekusukey Church; rejoicing, out here, folks soon will be.

Keystone pipeline rips a deep bleeding wound. The mourning river is running red.
No Trespassing sign declares if you're not arriving to exploit, out here you should not be.

Me and sister singing and telling old lies, cursing the living and praising the dead.
At brother's grave, the whiskey poured then hoisted. Out here, lawman, leave us be.

Boarded up main street, Seminole Nation. At Wind Clan allotment, gravehouses whisper shadow.
In cold rain under catalpas at freedman's Lima Town, quoting DuBois out here, as we should be.

Holdenville quick-stop is flooded with tweakers hoping meth is the cure for their sorrow.
Indian casino promises fortune but slots are nothing but noise. Out here, Luck will never be.

Tracing lines of resistance and sites of rebellion where farmers of The Green Corn bled.
Ghosts chant revolution in Sasakwa streets, their socialist voices out here, will forever be.

On this impossible day, a magic carpet ride with Djinni of the Crosstimbers and a dancing crow,
a rebel-gray sky is jealous of your eyes, of their verdigris joy, out here, where we cannot be.

Pia Toya
for Dustin

Tell me your story,
Shauna said, *this is how*
we say hello in Comanche.

You said yes,
there is a story
behind that story

and all night long,
over the clamoring
slots, we speak story

honoring our histories,
recognizing the web
of words story weaves,

spinning tales that bind
us, one tribe to another.
Years ago, Oren told me

all stories are true—
whether they happened
or not, is another matter.

Inside your heart
is a mountain written over
with a story not its own.

Let us remember its
ancient name, tell its true
story in the old way

made new.

The Quah Effect

for The Quah Crew: Faith, Murv, Debbie, & Cassandra

*In Tahlequah, time staggers. It halts, leaps, spins, and burrows down
into the rocky soil to remind us that everything that ever happened in
a place is happening still.*

Staggers isn't such a pretty idea.
Especially with Indians in the picture.
And Irish. And Scots.

All people who lean into drunkenness
as shadow leans into light.

Say instead: stutter steps.
Dance one forward, two back.
Sideways if you're feeling the
presence of haints and shades.

Or go ahead and live unvarnished.
Admit the ancestral jake leg,
drink until evening has to close
because the moon said so, flip the
bird to sun lurking on horizon,
pissed off and ready to make
your hangover worse.

It is happening. It is all happening.
How can you not feel it?
How can you not puke
with vertigo? History has not been well-
described. She's a bitch. A
Siren. A Medusa.

Don't trust her. You never
know what garments she'll wear
to your funeral.

*In Tahlequah, 24 hours is simultaneously a lifetime and a deep
breath.*

Deep breath.

Breathe.
It doesn't matter that you're suffocating.
Air is everything.
Lean into it.
Find the place where *stigini*
shimmer and screech.

Where your grandmother's life
was counted less than desire.

Where Catahoula-claw love-hickeys
appear on your thigh days later.

Where you have lived inside everyone's
myth but your own.

Dance. Trilling. Tattered shawl.

Follow this. Become this.

Lifetime.

Forget that your grandmother's rape
reenacted a thousand other rapes—

the white man
the colonial man
his privilege announcing
the dark woman his property.

Forget that your own rapes
have followed the same pattern.
That all rapes do.

Someone else has claimed you
planted their flag without your consent.

Not the horse but the horseless carriage.

Not the daytime raid but the late night invasion.

Not the scream but the shameful reentry
into the house that put you on the block.

Breathe deeply. Begin again.

Einstein must have heard tell of Tahlequah the day he thought up the space-time continuum—forever compressing, then expanding and exploding into a moment.

I am not a card holder.
Despite my grandmothers' petitions
I do not possess a Certificate of Degree of Indian Blood.

Some say I have no right to speak.
Of the ghosts. Of the terrors.

But it's all here, now.
In my head.
In my staggered gut.

In the loss of meaning.
In the loss. In the loss.
In the loss.

In the way time folds and unfolds
into my body as if it never wanted more
than to be taken.

Even the body lies.
Even the soul lies.

Only this second, this moment
tells stories, tells truths.

Circling around until we're wrapped up in its folded layers, like
children swaddled in a blanket.

This one day, I find a way back.

It is a temporary amnesia,
a momentary lapse of reason,
twenty-four hours of of of
peace.

Of comfort.

Of something I would have called
home.

Later, I wonder if I've fooled
myself or if it really happened

happening

still happening

always happening.

Re-entry into linear time is difficult and and painful—

What a joke. Time as
something that
something that
something that goes
along on its business

without

without ever
circling back around
circling

as we all know it does.

Fuck the marches of
time, spit on time strolling
down the aisles of history.

Time never walks betrothed down the aisle.
It's forever a bridesmaid never a bride.

It always sings in trumpet.
It never disappears behind
the last decade.

It's always lurking around
the corner, the corner
bar where the jukebox plays
oldies and desiccated men
who have been playing shuffleboard
there for decades wonder

who the hell are all these people
(*I don't know*)

and why have they gathered here?

. . . the clock time of late capitalism is a wobbly arrow falling without hitting its target, while all around and above and below it, Indian time—Cherokee County time, cottonwood and cottonmouth time, wolf time, river time—dances in turtle rattles across the milky way.

I have heard tell of a man
who said History could be analyzed.

History resists,
tells her story
through the mouths
of the winners

those who don't win, lose.

those who don't hunger, eat.

those who don't pray, curse.

those who don't work
own the labor of those who do.

But this is too metaphysical.
Or too material. Remind me
which is which.

It comes down to this:
head out for The Territories
east of the 97th parallel
south of the cultural Mason-Dixon

where there are two kinds of
survivors: the crackers and the
others—the music makers, the poets,
the artists, the medicine people.
I come from both kinds.

These ones, the occult resistance,
bring into being The Quah Effect:
a space-time continuum
you cannot enter unless invited.
You cannot leave unless
renounced.
You cannot forget unless
you're decomposing
in the dark forests
beneath a red cedar.

And then, and then
and then

the cedar cannot forget you.

The cottonwood lives on
your compost, the river carries
you away, the cottonmouth
snake secretes you as venom

and the turtle and the wolf
tell you a story about History
and how all that has happened—

you included

will happen, again.

In Tahlequah, time staggers. It halts, leaps, spins, and burrows down into the rocky soil to remind us that everything that ever happened in a place is happening still. Where 24 hours is simultaneously a lifetime and a deep breath. Einstein must have heard tell of Tahlequah the day he thought up the space-time continuum forever compressing, then expanding and exploding into a moment. circling around until we're wrapped up in its folded layers, like children swaddled in a blanket. Re-entry into linear time is difficult and and painful—the clock time of late capitalism is a wobbly arrow falling without hitting its target, while all around and above and below it, Indian time—Cherokee County time, cottonwood and cottonmouth time, wolf time, river time,—dances in turtle rattles across the milky way.

Glossary

"Not Quite Glengarry," page 11.
All the "character" names in the poem are taken from David Mamet's play (later film), *Glengarry Glen Ross*.

"Elemental Ceramics," pages 29-30.
This poem is patterned after ancient and medieval philosophy's "Five Essences" of the universe: earth, air, fire, and water, and the "highest" essence, quintessence.

"Sintered," refers to "sintering," "the process of compacting and forming a solid mass of material by heat and/or pressure without melting it to the point of liquefaction." See https://en.wikipedia.org/wiki/Sintering.

"That Summer," page 41.
This poem is in remembrance of the three girls raped and murdered at Camp Scott on June 13, 1977. The author was next door, at Camp Fire Camp Waluhili.

"Malissa, 1983," page 44.
A *descanso* is a roadside memorial to someone who died in a traffic accident, often seen in the Southwest.

"Driving Lost Roads Listening to Jedi Mind Tricks," pages 66-67.
"Farmers of The Green Corn" refers to the 1917 tri-racial, farmer-led Socialist uprising in southeast Oklahoma. The center of the Rebellion was Sasakwa, OK, 20 miles from the author's home town.

"*Pia Toya*," page 68.
Pia Toya is the Comanche name for Mt. Scott, a mountain in the center of Oklahoma's portion of Comancheria.

"The Quah Effect," pages 69-77.
"The Quah" is a local term for the town of Tahlequah, OK.

"Haints and shades" are two different kinds of noncorporeal presences.

"Jake leg," is a neurological disorder, usually expressed as hallucinations and a permanent partial paralysis of the feet, caused by poisoned whiskey. "Jake" comes from Jamaican ginger extract, a patent medicine that was 70-80% ethanol, which was often imbibed instead of difficult-to-procure liquor During Prohibition, the US government poisoned industrial alcohol, (used to make Jamaican Ginger) and whiskey (usually confiscated from illegal stills) with, among other deadly additives, methyl alcohol, kerosine, carbolic acid, and ortho-tri-cresyl phosphate, used in the leather and lacquer industries. "Jake leg" was first described by Oklahoma doctors Dr. Walter H. Miles and Dr. E. Goldfain, and reported in a March 7, 1930 front-page article in *The Oklahoman*. See http://newsok.com/article/3849680

"Stigini" is the Muscogee name for shape-shifting owl/humans who are generally considered harbingers of death among southern Native tribes; sometimes spelled "ishkitini."

"Catahoula" is the indigenous dog of North America bred by Native Americans, especially in the South. The word *catahoula* seems to be of Choctaw origin.

"The Territories" is another name for Oklahoma, referencing the "Twin Territories" of Indian Territory and Oklahoma Territory.

JEANETTA CALHOUN MISH is a poet, writer, and literary scholar. In 2015, Lamar University Press published Mish's first collection of prose, *Oklahomeland: Essays*. Her 2009 poetry collection, *Work Is Love Made Visible* (West End Press), won an Oklahoma Book Award, a Wrangler Award, and a WILLA Award from Women Writing the West. Her chapbook, *Tongue Tied Woman*, won the 2001 Edda Poetry Chapbook for Women contest sponsored by Sarasota Poetry Theater Press. Mish is a contributing editor for *Oklahoma Today* and *Sugar Mule: A Literary Journal*. She is founding editor of Mongrel Empire Press, which was recognized as 2012 Publisher of the Year by the Woodcraft Circle of Native Writers and Storytellers. Dr. Mish directs The Red Earth Creative Writing MFA program at Oklahoma City University where she also serves as a faculty mentor in writing pedagogy and the craft of poetry. More information and upcoming readings and events can be found on her website: www.tonguetiedwoman.com.